I Wish I Lived - WHEN NOAH DID

by
Geoffrey T. Bull
Illustrated by Chris Higham

Pickering
LONDON

Printed in Great Britain
ISBN 0 7208 2244-0
Cat. No. 11/3501

Copyrig... & Inglis Ltd. 1977

I sometimes wish a wish you know
Then all at once away I go
Across the ocean far and wide,
All tossed about by wind and tide!

It's kind of rough and wild out there;
Yet other times it's bright and fair.
I quite forget where land might be;
I'm like a bird, and just as free.
I love to fly instead of run,
Above the waves, beneath the sun,
Where bracing winds and salty breezes
Blow away one's coughs and sneezes!

One day I touched down in the sea
With quite a splash for little me!
I somehow kept myself afloat,
Then all at once I saw a boat.

It seemed so long, it looked so high,
Yet wasn't really sailing by,
It sort of wallowed in the waves;
I thought how strange this ship behaves!
Is no one there to make it go,
Or stop it rocking to and fro?

It had no oars and no propeller.
I thought perhaps I ought to hail her.
I saw no captain's bridge or gunwale
It did not even have a funnel.

No not a sail, a name or tag;
There was no mast; there was no flag.
Nor were there sailors on her deck
Yet this big ship was not a wreck.
It surely was the strangest boat
That anyone had seen afloat!

The water was not cold to me.
I'll have a swim, I thought, and see
Just what this boat is all about;
Then once I'm close I'll give a shout.

A big black bird came flying by;
My lips let out a little cry.
'I wish I knew about this boat
And how it keeps itself afloat.
I'd love to know who lives inside,
A ship so long and tall and wide!'

The raven looked at me and croaked,
'That's quite a story! My! You're soaked!
See now, the sun shines pleasantly,
So spread your wings and fly with me.
This boat', he said, 'is called the Ark.
Maybe, inside, you'd think it dark,
But there's a window in the roof.
Come fly this way. Look! There's the proof!

'Eight folk are shut in there you know.
God closed the door some months ago.
And there are lions and tigers too;
Enough wild beasts to make a zoo!'
'But why', I asked, 'are they together?
To save them from the stormy weather?'

'That's true and more,' the raven said.
'You see the world was very bad
And none but Noah, his wife and boys
Would listen to God's warning voice.
The things that men and women did,
Their sinful thoughts could not be hid.
God saw their evil day by day
And said, "They must be swept away!"

'But God is kind; He gave men time
Before He brought the flood and slime
Across the earth to punish sin.
"Repent!" He said, "and enter in
The Ark my servant Noah prepares.
Believe the witness that he bears!"'

Suddenly a little dove,
White as snow and on the move,
Flew towards us leaf in bill,
Lighted on the window-sill.

'What is this?' I dared to ask.
'Oh,' she said, 'you see my task
Is to bring the news to Noah
That God's anger is no more.
See the flood is going down;
By this leaf it's clearly shown
That the tree-tops may be seen
Where the waters once have been.'

When the passengers had heard
All the news brought by the bird;
Noah, his wife, Shem, Japheth, Ham
And their wives along with them
Felt so full of praise to God
Who had saved them from the flood.

Soon the hills, the rocks, the trees
Came to view, and by degrees
I could see a world washed clean,
Free from every trace of sin!

When upon Mount Ararat,
Finally the Ark had sat;
Once the waters drained away,
Then upon a sunny day
Out stepped Noah and all his 'crew';
Animals and reptiles too!

There and then they gathered stones,
Faithful Noah and all his sons.
'We must build an altar now;
Honour God, before Him bow,
Thank Him for the Ark He gave us.
Nothing but His Ark could save us!'

As the smoke rose to the sky,
I could see in heaven on high
All the colours of a rainbow,
Like an everlasting halo,
Round about the Throne of God,
Who had saved them from the flood.
Then a voice like many waters,
Sounded to His sons and daughters,
'I will not destroy again
All the world by flood and rain.'

For one flight, it was enough.
Then just like a piece of fluff,
Down I came, still floating down,
Clutching at my dressing-gown.